SEEING IT

—— HIS ——

WAY

SEEING IT
— HIS —
WAY

40 NIGHTS
WITH A CHRISTIAN
POLICE OFFICER

STEPHEN MATTICE

TATE PUBLISHING & *Enterprises*

Published by Tate Publishing & Enterprises, LLC
127 E. Trade Center Terrace | Mustang, Oklahoma 73064 USA
1.888.361.9473 | www.tatepublishing.com

Tate Publishing is committed to excellence in the publishing industry. The company reflects the philosophy established by the founders, based on Psalm 68:11,
"The Lord gave the word and great was the company of those who published it."

Book design copyright © 2010 by Tate Publishing, LLC. All rights reserved.
Cover design by Amber Gulilat
Interior design by Scott Parrish

Published in the United States of America

ISBN: 978-1-61663-628-9
1. Religion, Christian Life, Devotional
2. Religion, Christian Life, Spiritual Growth
10.07.15

DEDICATION

This book is dedicated first and foremost to Jesus Christ, the one who rescued me, preserved me, and saved my soul.

I also want to dedicate this book to my dad, Dr. Howard Mattice. Without him, none of this ever would have been possible.

This book is also dedicated to my lovely wife, Nanette, who has been a steady source of encouragement throughout this endeavor.

Finally, this book is dedicated to my three wonderful children, listed from oldest to youngest: Pierce, Emma, and Benjamin. I pray that each of you will always strive to see things God's way.

FOREWORD

The author, who is a reflective thinker, has had a flair for writing dating back to his childhood. Employing this writing talent for the Lord's work is a new venture for him. It began when his maturing Christian mind-set reflected upon his daily encounters with individuals whose societal values permitted them to engage in activities outside of the accepted norm. Secular thinking police officers tend to see only the actions of the offending individual and their responsibility to deal with the matter in accordance to law. The author shares their view of the proper legal action to be employed against law breakers. He also sees the reality that these are individuals for whom Christ died and understands the difference between their current behavior and their possibilities of change, should they embrace Christ and his salvation.

Having been a police officer for several years, he began to reflect upon his experiences with individuals and situations. As he thought on his experiences, he decided to write some of them down and to make a positive Christian reflection with respect to them. He has often shared his thoughtful writing with me over the telephone. I asked him to mail me several essays from his collection so that I could read them and contemplate upon what he was saying. As I read, I reached a conclusion: these short essays should be published so that his insights could be shared with others. It is hoped that, through reading these reflective accounts, others will gain a greater appreciation of the work of Christian police officers and that they will pray for them and for the needs of those with whom they must deal, that Christ might get the glory out of difficult situations.

Howard L. Mattice, Ed.D.
Professor of Education and History
Clearwater Christian College

Author's note:
This foreword was written by my father approximately two months before the Lord called him home to heaven. This book is a memorial to him and his years of ministry, as well as a continuation of the work which Christ began in me as a result of my father's influence.

INTRODUCTION

When I was asked by a pastor to share my testimony for the Wednesday night service, I initially reflected on what kind of grand revelation I could share by the story of my life and what amazing truths I could enlighten the congregation with by my words. Then, when I returned to reality, I became grateful for the opportunity. I decided it was best to learn from my past mistakes and ask God what it was he wanted me to say. I vowed that I would say nothing more and nothing less than what God wanted me to say. It is important for us to remember that we are merely the instruments through which God produces his works, and we must be willing and humble to obey his commands, going only where he sends us and speaking only what he tells us to speak. The servant is not greater than the master.

The introduction to this book is a portion of the message I shared on that night in church. The Lord drew my attention to this account in Acts 19:11–17 (NIV):

God did extraordinary miracles through Paul, so that even handkerchiefs and aprons that had touched him were taken to the sick, and their illnesses were cured and the evil spirits left them. Some Jews who went around driving out evil spirits tried to invoke the name of the Lord Jesus over those who were demon-possessed. They would say, "In the name of Jesus, whom Paul preaches, I command you to come out." Seven sons of Sceva, a Jewish chief priest, were doing this. (One day) the evil spirit answered them, "Jesus I know, and I know about Paul, but who are you?" Then the man who had the evil spirit jumped on them and overpowered them all. He gave them such a beating that they ran out of the house naked and bleeding. When this became known to the Jews and Greeks living in Ephesus, they were all seized with fear, and the name of the Lord Jesus was held in high honor.

This was an interesting report of people performing with potentially good intentions, but acting out of the will of God. These were people attempting to do God's work without the power of God behind them.

So what does this have to do with my personal story?

The Bible tells us that the Word of God is sharper than any two-edged sword. We wouldn't allow our children to play with knives or sharp objects. They would only hurt themselves. Perhaps, in joking around with someone, you have heard one person say to another, "I better do that for you. You'll end up hurting yourself." The same applies to individuals claiming to be doing God's work while they are out of the will of God and without the power of God behind them. And this is where my story comes in.

I grew up in New York City. My parents were very strong Christians, very involved in the Baptist Church. My father had been a pastor of a church in Brooklyn, and both he and my mother taught Sunday school. By the time I was twelve years old, I could quote by memory more Scripture than most people could in a lifetime. At a quarter for new verses and ten cents a verse for previously learned Scripture, my parents allowed me to earn my allowance. In time, I was able to recite entire books such as Ephesians, Philippians, and James, various scattered chapters of the Bible, and countless Psalms and individual verses. In church, my brother and I were considered to be well-behaved, highly intelligent children. We knew all of the answers in Sunday school, and could sing along to any song. We both played musical instruments, and could play the entire hymnbook and knew many of the words of the hymns by heart.

But I overlooked the love of God and saw him as a God of anger and vengeance. Some of the most enthusiastic, hellfire and brimstone sermons I have ever heard preached were given by none other than my mother—at the kitchen table after dinner. By the time I was eight, I was sure that I was one of the worst sinners on the face of the earth, and was facing certain condemnation in hell if I didn't change my sinful ways. This is the God I became acquainted with, and I feared him. Many times, I prayed to God to save me and to change me, because I didn't want to go to hell when I died. Salvation was fire insurance.

As I grew older, the love of Christ was a foreign concept to me. A relationship with Jesus was something that I did not know anything about, and wasn't sure I really wanted. Christian people were boring, weird, and judgmental, and their parents didn't let them wear cool clothes. Church was boring, Christian music was boring, church people were boring, annoying, and fake, and God was boring. It was easy for me to walk away, and I did.

Although I continued to walk away from God, he continued to remind me of his presence. I did my best to ignore him. The entertainment of the world became my addiction, and I lived from one excitement to the next. My God was rock music, and it was here that I turned for all of my answers. The harder I tried to ignore God, the heavier my rock music became. The more I tried to shut out his voice, the louder my rock music became, until I shut him out completely.

Through the years, like the people of Israel in the Old Testament, I occasionally turned to God whenever things got really bad. Out of guilt, I attempted to prove to God that I could still serve him and would try to pay back a little of what I felt I owed him. But anything I wanted to do for God had to be about me. I'm not much for watching TV, but there's a show on television about a great doctor with a big ego and a real arrogant attitude, named Dr. House. In one episode, this doctor began keeping score of how many things were the results of his work, and how many were because of God's intervention. In a way, I guess that's how I was. I did not want to join in a work already in progress; I always wanted to start something new because I felt surely God would use me to change the entire world. This behavior usually impressed people. I looked good to Christians. To pastors, I appeared to be on fire for the Lord. And—just like the ones in Acts 19 who acted out of God's will—I tried to force things to happen, even outwardly attempting to give God the glory for these things in an effort to prove to others that he was working in my life. The truth was that God was in my head. He had never been in my heart. I had the knowledge of God. I knew the Bible. I had heard the sermons. I knew how to talk the talk; but I was just like the guys trying to cast out the demons … and it was useless. And every time the first temptation of sin came my way, I gave in to it and walked away again.

But walking away from God is costly, and I am sure that I hurt many lives in the process. There is no need to drag up all of the dirt and turn it into a bragging session of how sinful I was, for that serves no purpose. I thank God that he gave sight to my spiritually blind eyes.

One day, I began seeking the friendship of a youth pastor. He explained to me that Christianity wasn't about the rules; it was about a relationship with Jesus. For the first time in my life, a light bulb turned on in my dark mind, and I thought I finally understood the meaning of true Christianity. I prayed that, if God kept his promises, then I wanted to know the truth, and I wanted the truth to set me free, just like he promised it would.

That very night, when I prayed that prayer, I felt like I was on fire. I felt that I had just had my first real encounter with the true God. And once again, I set out to prove that I could do anything for him. My youth pastor friend encouraged me to find where God was at work and join that effort. He told me that I should stop trying to reinvent the wheel and to stop going out on my own, where there was no support from an already working network of Christians. For a few weeks, I assisted him on Wednesday nights at the teen youth meetings. Then the ideas came again, and once more it became all about me and what I could do for God. I came up with, and even followed through with, ideas for street ministry. I even developed an outlined program for following up on teenagers who had just accepted Christ, in order to keep them involved in church.

I should have taken my own advice. It was about my ego. It was about acceptance. I wanted the praise. I wanted the recognition. I wanted to feel the approval of other Christians, and my head grew a few sizes larger every time attention was drawn to my accomplishments. It inflated my ego to have someone ask me to do something important. I remember thinking, *I don't see any ways that the devil can get to me now; there are no cracks in my Christian armor.*

Little did I realize it, but Satan was using my own good intentions to bring me down to failure and defeat. I was sincere, but I was sincerely wrong. I was acting out of the will of God, without the power of God behind me. I made sure to make it look as if I was on fire for God, and drew attention to the fact that surely others needed to be encouraged by me to do the same. I made it seem as if I was a strong man of God, looking for others to do what I was doing. And when another church asked me to be their youth leader, I foolishly accepted.

Once again, instead of joining God in his work, I was sure I needed a leadership role. And when I went off on my own, I think God finally said, "Okay, Stephen. Go ahead. You'll learn." When I failed miserably, I turned like a spoiled brat child and ran away. If God was on this side of the universe, I was going to be on the other. It didn't matter. He obviously wasn't interested in anything I was doing anyway. And once again, I gave up. This time, it was for three years.

I was acting out of the will of God, and certainly did not have the power of God behind me. If ever there was a recipe for absolute failure—that would be it. Then one day, when I grew tired of running away, I began to feel the Spirit of God asking me if I was done running. I told him that I wasn't, and continued to do my own thing, while every day wrestling with God, trying hard to silence his voice. But you cannot silence the voice of God.

Jesus says he stands at the door of your heart and knocks. The only thing you need to do is to let him in. Pray and ask him to come into your life. And if you ask him to, he will take control, and will direct your life and make it everything it was ever intended to be. And then, just like me, you will ask yourself, "Why didn't I do this a long time ago?"

In Sunday school, we sing the song, "I have decided to follow Jesus, No turning back." The truth of the matter is this: Salvation is sincerely accepting Jesus Christ, truly giving control of your life to God. It requires praying to God, accepting his forgiveness for every sin you ever committed, and asking him to make you into a new person. He will help you to change; and sometimes the change is gradual as the Holy Spirit draws your attention to various areas of your life. If you are obedient to his leading and have really decided to follow Jesus, then there is no turning back. If you recited a prayer that was nothing more than words, and there has been *no change* in your thoughts, desires, or actions—then you are not a Christian. The word *Christian* means to be like Christ. Christ acted only in the will of God with the power of God behind him.

I can tell you that when I finally surrendered my life to God, he took over my will. When I gave my heart to Christ, then the power of God was in me and was able to change me and motivate me to do his will, not mine. My highest desire is that God will use me to bring unsaved people one step closer to his kingdom, in whatever method the Lord chooses to use me.

Sometimes I sow the seeds, sometimes I water them, but only God knows when the harvest is ready. It is my mission to be available for every task the Lord makes known to me, and only to move when he gives the command. Just as a police officer is to be the servant of the people, I am a servant of God.

It is my prayer that the Lord will help me to see the world his way. As a police officer, it becomes obvious to me every day that Christ is the only answer to all of the problems of this world. We must see the people and the events of everyday life as opportunities in a mission field, where lessons can be learned for spiritual growth. I challenge you to ask God to use you as a missionary in your workplace, and in your daily life. He needs people in all professions. Ask him for a new perspective of the world around you, so that you begin to see it his way.

CHAPTER ONE

So, if you think you are standing firm, be
careful that you don't fall!

1 Corinthians 10:12 (NIV)

I listened intently as my fellow officer told me about
the arrest he had made earlier that afternoon. He went
into detail about the extremely drunken state of the
six foot one, very large man, who was in the middle of
fighting with his frightened wife. The man was angry
that the police had been called, and yelled at the officer, "You're going to need all the back-up you can get!"
After a physical confrontation over the couch and onto
the floor, and a painful encounter with police O.C.
pepper spray, the suspect finally gave up resisting arrest,
just as back-up arrived at the front door of the residence. The struggle was over, and the man was taken
into custody for domestic battery and resisting arrest.

When I saw the report, I immediately recognized the man as one who fairly regularly attended church and who made efforts to make sure his family attended as well. Many thoughts went through my head, but fortunately, God had taught me personal lessons about passing judgment on others. There was a time in my life where I had said to myself, "I don't see any way that the devil can get to me now. There are no cracks in my Christian armor." These thoughts preceded three years of desperately running from God, avoiding church, and living a life as a poster child for the devil's kingdom. When I thought that I stood firm like a rock, and became confident in my own strength, the slightest breeze of temptation made me stumble and fall.

I am thankful that, for those who have faith in Christ, there is forgiveness for sins, restoration for unfaithfulness, and a welcome home party prepared by God himself for the prodigal sons and daughters. I am reminded of a Christian song, which stated that even if we walk 10,000 steps away from Jesus, it's still only one step back. All we have to do is ask him to return us to his flock, and he will.

CHAPTER TWO

Cast all your anxiety on Him because He cares for you.

1 Peter 5:7

I work full-time midnight shifts from 11 p.m. to 7 a.m. Sometimes, if things are quiet and the streets are deserted, it allows me time to think as I patrol through the side roads and back alleys. This can be a great time to talk to God in prayer, listen to music, or turn the volume up on a good song on the radio. It can also be a time of turmoil and trouble, as the concerns of the daytime world sneak in and slowly try to weigh me down. If I'm not careful, concern can turn into worry. Worry then can turn into anxiety, wondering how to work out certain circumstances.

Financial problems, work related issues, family matters ... the list of things which can cause anxiety goes on and on. Many times I have expressed frustration because I want to handle a problem immediately, but I have to wait until morning. Sometimes, this means I have to work through my entire midnight shift before I have the opportunity to settle a financial or family difficulty. Then there's an arrest right before the end of my shift, causing me to work a few hours later. It's much easier to handle drunk drivers, domestic disputes, and help civilians work through their problems when my own world is free of stress. But that isn't how things are in the real world.

Christ said that we can give all of our problems to him and that he will take care of them for us, if we truly allow him to do so. The hardest thing for me to do, it seems, is to let go of life's daily problems and allow God to handle them. My prayer every day needs to be that God will teach me to trust him more and more. I am confident that he will not allow me to drown in the midst of difficulty. Jesus told the disciples that a sparrow doesn't fall from the sky without God knowing about it. What a great thought! As the hymn says, "His eye is on the sparrow, and I know He watches me." Lord, help us to cast our cares on you.

CHAPTER THREE

But in your hearts set apart Christ as Lord. Always be prepared to give an answer to everyone who asks you to give the reason for the hope that you have.

1 Peter 3:15

I was sent to a house one night where a fight and a break-in had taken place. The suspect was still at the house when I arrived, sitting on the floor, badly battered, both eyes swollen, drunk, and bleeding. Hours later, after he ceased being combative, he began to speak to me. I had dealt with this same subject numerous times in similar situations. He told me that I was the only one he trusted and that he did not understand why I was continuously so understanding of him. I told him that that was a conversation we would have to have someday.

When I arrived at the local hospital with him, I felt compelled to invite him to church. He immediately responded that he would love to go to church and that he felt it was something he needed to do. I knew that God was prompting me to plant a seed there. Perhaps I would be the one to water the seed as well; maybe it would be someone else. One way or the other, it would be God who would reap the harvest. Regardless of the outcome, I knew God wanted me to let him know that any kindness or understanding was a result of Christ living in me and through me.

I don't make a habit of giving people gospel tracts while on duty, but I keep one in my police bag for the rare occasion in which I can give one to someone while at work. Part of our job is to offer help to people in whatever way seems necessary. Jesus Christ is the only hope for someone trapped in destructive behaviors. I realize that we cannot preach sermons to people, and the nature of most employment does not allow for witnessing to people about Christ. But if we keep our eyes and ears open, and if we pray for the opportunity to do so, God will provide a circumstance where we can share him as the reason for the hope within us.

CHAPTER FOUR

With the tongue we praise our Lord and
Father, and with it we curse men, who have
been made in God's likeness.

James 3:9

When I asked God for a short message to add to the
devotional today, he had a message directly for me
instead. I have already learned that a wise response to
the Word of the Lord is twofold: listen and obey.

Police officers are not perfect people. But, because
we tend to hold the world to a higher standard of conduct, it only makes sense that we almost expect perfection from each other. When that standard of conduct is
broken, it is sad to watch coworkers turn on each other
and point fingers. This scenario occurred at a department where I worked.

A fellow police officer had violated the standard
code of conduct expected from members of our pro-

fession. Instead of offering assistance to the officer, it seemed that some members of the department had turned into wolves, ready to move in for the kill on the one who had done wrong. Others, although quieter, growled and bared their teeth from a distance. I found myself in the middle of all of it and was just as guilty as the rest of the wolf pack. I was angry about the entire situation. I was angry with my fellow officer; I was angry at the administration for not handling the incident in the way that I was sure was best. I had become a poor example of a Christian in this regard.

It is impossible to offer praise and worship to God the Father while we verbally hold a fellow man in contempt. We cannot bless the name of the Lord and call down judgment on a coworker. First of all, we must remember that God says he is the judge. Secondly, it is our responsibility to pick someone up who has fallen and help him back to his feet. Perhaps this is what the police chief had in mind when he wrote on our message board: Men who live in glass houses should not throw stones!

CHAPTER FIVE

So if the Son sets you free, you will be free indeed.

John 8:36

I stopped a pick-up truck early one morning because it did not have working tail lights. When I approached the vehicle, I noticed that the inside of the truck smelled like old marijuana. The driver was known for having drugs, and his passenger was a well known methamphetamine cook. A search of the vehicle, with the help of a K9, did not yield any illegal substance, and the two drove off with nothing more than a citation for not having proof of current insurance.

A few minutes later, as a result of this stop, I began thinking about addictions. The world has set a standard of what appears to be acceptable and non-acceptable addictions. Drug addictions, whether prescription or illegal, are seen as a societal abomination in today's world. Alcohol addiction is commonly accepted, as long as certain anti-social behaviors do not result. Yet the world tends to ignore the addictions that plague the soul. Lustful thoughts, indecent conversation, laziness, inappropriate language ... the list could go on and on.

We, as law enforcement officers, put behaviors into categories and give the consequences a misdemeanor or felony ranking system. God sees sin for exactly what it is—the actions that prompted him to send his Son, Jesus Christ, to die so that we don't have to spend an eternity in separation from him. God cannot look on sin. He does not label any of our self-destructive behaviors or addictions as acceptable, even if they may seem harmless to the rest of the world around us.

I thank God that Jesus Christ died to set us free from all of our sins, addictions, and harmful behaviors. These things cannot hold us as captives because Christ has the power, if we ask, to break any chains of bondage and set us free. True victory can only come from Jesus.

CHAPTER SIX

You know very well that the day of the
Lord will come like a thief in the night.

1 Thessalonians 5:2

For the most part, I patrol in the police car by myself.
One night, I had another officer with me. About 1 a.m.,
he received a call from his wife. She was terrified, having just come eye to eye through a window of their
house with someone who had broken into their front
porch enclosure. When she yelled, the thief dropped
the chain saw he was attempting to steal and ran.
Within seconds, I dropped the officer off a block from
his house, so he could search the immediate area on
foot and check on his wife, while I continued to spot-
light the streets and alleys. Additional units responded,
as we tried in vain to find the intruder. Even with the
help of a K9, the efforts proved to be fruitless. The
thief had disappeared just as quickly as he had arrived.

The day will come when Jesus Christ will return to take every believer from this earth, both living and dead. It will come quickly, unexpectedly, and will take place quicker than we can blink an eye. There will be no time to say a prayer; there will be no time to accept Christ while he is in the act of returning. For those who stated that they just weren't ready to receive Christ, or that they would do it another day, their window of opportunity will be closed. As of that point, there are no second chances. To add to the despair, each person left behind will vividly remember in desperate anguish every opportunity that they ever had to accept God's free gift of salvation. I thank God that I will not be among them. But more importantly, I pray that God will give me a chance every day to tell someone about him, in hopes that they will not be counted among the lost the day Christ returns.

CHAPTER
SEVEN

There is a time for everything, and a season
for every activity under heaven: a time to be
born and a time to die...

Ecclesiastes 3:1–2A

There is a busy section of highway that runs through
the city where I work and live. In the last year, there
have been several deaths on this highway from colli-
sions involving passenger cars and large semi trucks.
Although I have seen death many times and in many
forms, I cannot escape the incredible reality of the
scene when I arrive. It is very humbling to know that
an individual is now in their place of eternal destiny.
Sometimes this happens very suddenly and violently, as
in the case of horrific traffic accidents.

Many times I have been at the scene of a fatal accident where, although the person is no longer living, the
watch on their wrist continues to tick away the sec-

onds and minutes. It is a sight of absolute irony. Time is over for one; time continues for another. Time has no respect of persons.

Normally, within seconds of arriving at a fatality, even as I perform the duties which my law enforcement job requires, my mind has already questioned where the person's soul is at that very moment. I wonder if the person knew Jesus Christ. I wonder if the person is currently enjoying the splendor of the lights of heaven, or if that individual passed from the nighttime of this world into the never ending darkness of hell. Either way, time here on earth for that person has been completed. The time to give an account to God has begun.

The decisions we make while we are here on earth affect where our souls will spend eternity. Heaven or hell is a simple choice. Salvation is a free gift from God. All we need to do is ask Christ to save us, and to come into our lives and hearts to change us. It is important that we tell every person we can about this free gift of God, because not one of us knows the number of days or hours we have until our season is over. I don't want anyone to die without having a relationship with Jesus Christ.

CHAPTER EIGHT

For the wages of sin is death, but the gift of God is eternal life through Jesus Christ our Lord.

Romans 6:23

It was almost three o'clock in the morning, and I was patrolling near the high school. I noticed a car approaching the intersection without any headlights. As I turned the police car around to stop the vehicle, the driver began to speed up in an effort to get away from me. As we headed southbound out of the city limits, I began calling out the details of my pursuit to the county dispatcher. Soon the suspect vehicle was nearly at 100 miles per hour and had turned all of its lights off in an attempt to lose me in the dark. The driver was running through stop signs and swerving all over the road in an effort to maintain control. My sergeant instructed me to back off of the pursuit and return to the city. Difficult as it was for me to accept the command, I did as I was ordered and discontinued the chase. The car disappeared into the darkness.

As we know, sometimes high speed pursuits end up in disaster and death as a result of drivers losing control of their vehicles. Sometimes, they make desperate attempts at being elusive and become unbelievably careless, causing fatal accidents. The victim isn't always the suspect. Sometimes innocent lives, both civilian and law enforcement, are claimed in fatal car crashes.

The driver I chased that night foolishly put his own life in jeopardy and recklessly chose to endanger the lives of innocent others. Why? Perhaps he had a warrant for his arrest and didn't want to return to jail. Maybe he was under the influence of alcohol or drugs, or both. Possibly, he was attempting to get away because there were drugs in his car. There are many answers. Unfortunately, I was not able to find out that answer on that night. But the one thing I am sure of is that the driver's careless behavior, if continued, would most certainly have led to destruction and possibly even death.

Sin always leads to death. The flames of sin often begin as small sparks. But the spark ignites a flame that grows larger and larger, until it completely engulfs a person. God promises us that sin leads to death, but he also offers an alternative. The alternative is life through Jesus Christ. Jesus can break the chains of sin and set the condemned prisoner free. All we need to do is to ask him for this freedom.

I am thankful every day that Jesus Christ died on the cross to pay the price for my sin, so that, even when I pass through death as a human, I can have everlasting life with him in heaven.

CHAPTER NINE

Go into all the world and preach the good
news to all creation.

Mark 16:15

I remember the day I heard the message on my answering machine from a police chief offering me my first job as a police officer. I was excited and couldn't wait to get to work. On my first day, I completed all of the preliminary procedures, such as gathering uniforms, filling out paperwork, and swearing in as an officer to protect the city. I finally had a commission.

Many police departments do not allow their officers to hold a double commission working for another department or as an officer in another state. However, it occurred to me one day that, as a Christian police officer, I already have a double commission. My first and most important commission, known as the Great Commission, came from Christ when he commanded us to tell the entire world about him. My second commission is to enforce the laws of the jurisdiction I was given as a police officer.

Both commissions require boldness, courage, strength, and an attitude that is unwilling to back down in the face of an adversary. Sometimes both commissions demand that I go into places and situations where I do not want to go. Both commissions require me to be mindful of my words and behavior everywhere I go, because I am seen by the world as a representative of the one who commissioned me. In both commissions, I am held accountable to a higher authority, who oversees my actions and decisions.

Most importantly, both commissions remind me that I am never off duty.

CHAPTER
TEN

A man's own folly ruins his life...

Proverbs 19:3A

It had to be one of the most unbelievable things I had ever been sent to as a police officer; in fact, I can still hardly believe it. It was nearly 3 a.m. on a Monday morning. The police and sheriff dispatch center sent me to the scene of a truck fire. When I arrived, I found a group of people in a complete panic. The man who flagged me down asked me, out of breath, if I had a fire extinguisher. I told him that I didn't, but that the fire department was also en route. I parked and asked the group where the fire was; they told me their pick-up truck was on fire. I did not see any flames, so I asked, "Where?"

They responded, "It must have gone out." Then they explained to me what had happened. Apparently, the three men there were trying to siphon gasoline from one tank of a dual tank pick-up truck into the other tank of the same truck. Being dark outside, they needed a light source to brighten their activity. They chose to have a member of the group hold a cigarette lighter close to the gas tank in order to accomplish this task! Fortunately for all of them, the fumes did not ignite, but a small amount of splashed fuel surrounding the entrance of the gas tank caught fire and quickly was extinguished. This was an act of incredible folly, which could easily have ruined all of their lives.

The sinful pleasures of this world can also be labeled as folly. Sexual immorality, drug and alcohol abuse, gambling addictions, and many behaviors which constitute an unhealthy lifestyle can all be considered folly. In truth, anything that keeps your heart and mind from dedication to Christ is folly, and folly will ruin not only your life, but possibly, your eternity.

CHAPTER ELEVEN

The King will reply, "I tell you the truth, whatever you did for the least of these brothers of mine, you did for me."

Matthew 25:40

It was a cold night. As I entered a section of the city near the railroad tracks and some abandoned structures, I noticed the unmistakable smell of a dead body. I radioed dispatch and told them that I would be investigating the area to find the source of the odor, and I was informed that additional units would be on the way to help me.

I found the front door of an abandoned house standing wide open. This was the same house where, approximately two years earlier, the severely decayed body of a man had been found several days after his demise, in the middle of the summer heat.

This was probably the first time since that incident that the door of the house had been opened, because the residence had been closed up after the end of the death investigation. The house had remained shut and vacant for two years, trapping in the intense odor of the deceased until the door was opened once again on this night.

The two-year-old aroma was emitting strongly from within the house. Not knowing what or who I would find, I drew my gun and flashlight and stepped inside of the front door. With my first step inside of the house, my light fell upon the face of a vagrant woman, probably in her fifties, sitting upright and awake. She had been sleeping on a mattress, just inside of the front door.

I transported the woman to the police department, and attempted for several hours to find assistance for her. None of her family wished to help her or give her a place to stay. The social institutions I contacted stated that the situation did not warrant their services. I was unable to contact the local church organization, which usually paid for a one night stay at a hotel for a person in this state of need. The city in which I worked did not have an ordinance prohibiting vagrancy; so even the jail was not an option.

After trying every possibility unsuccessfully, I reluctantly told the woman that I had nothing to offer other than to tell her that she was free to leave. The verse above came to my mind as she turned to leave, and I decided to obey the prompting inside of my head. I rarely give money to anyone without knowing what they would use it for, but I made an exception to my policy and handed the woman a twenty dollar bill. As we stepped outside, I noticed that the weather was too cold in comparison to what she was wearing. I had a warm sweatshirt inside of my personal vehicle, and I gave it to her. She thanked me for everything, put the sweatshirt on, and walked away. I sincerely wished that I could have done more to help.

It is not feasible to treat everyone this way, but when the Lord prompts us to do so, it is best to listen. I realize that often people falsely claim to be in need and will misuse the charity given to them. I also realize that many people who claim to be in poverty, holding up signs asking for our help, are merely abusing the system and taking advantage of the kindness of others. But this is not always the case. Fortunately, God knows our hearts. He knows that we cannot always distinguish between those in honest need and those who are not, but it is the attitude of our heart and our willingness to give and help others that he will reward.

CHAPTER TWELVE

God is our refuge and strength, an ever present help in trouble.

Psalm 46:1

Every law enforcement officer will, sooner or later, encounter an individual who will attempt to find whatever means he can to get out of trouble. Whether attempting to avoid a ticket or to sidestep an inevitable arrest, there are many who will do whatever it takes in order not to reap the consequences of their actions. This bargaining is sometimes used as a tool by police in order to learn about more criminal activity, such as drug dealing and manufacturing or gang related incidents.

It is extremely interesting to watch an individual in this type of circumstance, as he turns on his friends and acquaintances. The same people they partied and associated with, sometimes minutes before, are now nothing more to them than names which they can throw out in order to save themselves from the inconvenience of a ticket or jail time. Friends will turn on friends, and enemies will pretend to be friends so they can learn vital information to hand over to the police. The world of confidential informants has a solid foundation built on the principles of deception, double-crossing, and trickery. This often adds to the extreme paranoia of illegal drug users, dealers, and manufacturers. It is an unwritten rule among them that no one is to be trusted, and anyone, at anytime, could be an informant. There are no real friends in this realm.

I am thankful that God has always been faithful, even when I have not been faithful to him. I am glad that he has been a friend to me during good times and bad. I have never had to worry that God would turn his back on me or be two-faced. God said from the beginning that he is the great "I AM," which simply means that he will never change. God is my refuge when I cannot seem to get away from the temptations of sin. God is my strength when I am weak. God will not turn on me in times of trouble. Thank you, God, for being the "friend who sticks closer than a brother."

CHAPTER THIRTEEN

Why do you fight and argue among your-
selves? Isn't it because of your sinful long-
ings? They fight inside you.

James 4:1

There are several bars in the immediate area where I
work and quite a few more in the surrounding areas.
Usually, on nights when the bars are open, I can count
on an alcohol related incident. This often occurs in
the form of a fight. It seems that the most consistent
underlying cause for disputes has something to do with
jealousy over a member of the opposite sex. Men fight
over women; women fight over men. Many times, the
fights are over inappropriate or sinful relations.

It seems that many destructive behaviors and hab-
its tend to lead to other destructive behaviors. It is not
uncommon to see the same people attend a night club
or bar as if it is a second home. The devastating effects

that this has on families are staggering. The average drunk driver will operate a vehicle approximately seventy times a year while under the influence of alcohol. The death and injury statistics from drunk driving are no surprise to anyone. Many of the fights and domestic disputes I am called to are a result of drunken quarrels after bar closing time.

Obviously, alcohol abuse is not the only reason for fighting and arguing. But, in law enforcement, if the call comes in after 2 a.m., the odds are greatly in the favor of it being alcohol related.

Christ offers a solution for those who wish to walk away from the paths of destruction. Joy, peace, and forgiveness are characteristics of an individual who has surrendered his life to the Lord. He can replace fighting and struggle with kindness and an encouraging spirit.

Every day, we need to pray that God will forgive and remove all of our sinful ways and help us to act and think more like Jesus. It is a lifelong process.

CHAPTER FOURTEEN

For God does not show favoritism.

Romans 2:11

I arrested a man for DUI on a Saturday night. In Kansas, DUI means Driving Under the Influence, whether it is alcohol, drugs, or both. DUI in Kansas is a mandatory arrest, as is domestic battery. The law of the state of Kansas does not allow a police officer to exercise discretion concerning whether or not to arrest a drunk driver.

As the man was getting into the back of the police car, he said to me, "You're not from around here, are you? I've lived here my whole life." Over the course of the next half hour, he attempted to suggest that I should show him favoritism and not take him to jail for several reasons. In addition to the defense of being a long-term local, he stated that he went to school with the sheriff and knew him well. I responded that, perhaps if he and the sheriff were friends, he should give the sheriff a call in the morning. I also reminded him that it didn't matter if the police department's sergeant or chief were there at the time, the arrest would still have happened. The law does not care who a person knows or how popular they are in the local society.

God is the same way. The only thing that will matter when a person dies will be whether or not he has asked Jesus Christ to save him from his sins and forgive him for his wrongdoings. A sinner cannot enter heaven's gates because God cannot look upon sin. But a person who has asked Jesus to forgive him for every sin, and make him into a new person, is no longer in the sinner category; now he is in the forgiven and saved-by-grace category. This is the only way that a person may enter into heaven.

The Bible says clearly that there is no other way into heaven, except through accepting the death and resurrection of Jesus Christ for forgiveness of sins and salvation. It will not matter to God what church an individual belongs to; it won't matter what pastor or priest a person knows. It will not matter to God what good deeds a person has done or how much money he has, or what prayers or verses or Bible stories he has memorized, or how faithful he may have been to the laws of his religion. God will not show favoritism to any of these things.

God will only allow someone into heaven whose life and soul have been changed and saved by accepting Jesus Christ by praying to Him, "God, I am a sinner. I ask for your forgiveness for every sin I have ever committed, and pray that you will forgive me and save me, and make me into a new person. I accept Jesus Christ as the only way to enter into heaven. Help me to be the person you need me to be, and bring people into my life who will help me serve you and learn more about you. I pray this in the name of Jesus, Amen."

CHAPTER FIFTEEN

You will keep in perfect peace, him whose
mind is steadfast, because he trusts in you.

Isaiah 26:3

I was called out to a residence one night because a
mother was having problems with her daughter. When
I arrived, the daughter was incoherent, under the influence of illegal drugs. She had a severe problem with
methamphetamine usage and kept company with others of the same mind. I brought her outside of the
house in order to gain control of her without destroy-
ing the living room. She resisted and ended up lying on
the grass in the front yard, screaming and making loud,
strange noises. Her eyes rolled, and she began speaking unintelligibly in a low, grumbling, guttural voice,
while making slashing gestures across her throat. She
stuck out her tongue and made choking sounds, while
continuing the throat slashing movements. I called for

EMS, but felt as if I was looking upon an individual under demonic influence.

I have heard firsthand accounts of people who have had demonic encounters while using meth, crack, and other illegal substances. The human mind is powerful, yet vulnerable. Fantastically designed by God, the human brain can achieve outstanding wonders. But if abused and mistreated, the mind can be a tool of destruction for the devil to overcome the senses with terror and even insanity.

All of us have heard the expression that idle hands are the devil's workshop. The mind is no different. It is important that we use our minds to meditate on the things of God. The images, sounds, and activities with which we fill our brain capacities will either influence our behavior in a godly, positive direction, or lead us down the paths of destruction and fear. It is most important that we look at the world through the eyes of Christ and keep our minds on the things of God, who will keep us in perfect peace.

CHAPTER SIXTEEN

Anyone, then, who knows the good he
ought to do and doesn't do it, sins.

James 4:17

In law enforcement, in order to charge someone with a
specific crime, the suspect's criminal actions have to meet
the state statute's definition of that crime. Often, a decid-
ing factor is something called *criminal intent*. Words such
as *intentionally, willfully, recklessly, maliciously,* etc. are
examples of criminal intent. The basic principle of these
words suggests that the person had knowledge that the
crime they were committing was wrong, yet they chose to
do it anyway, in spite of the potential consequences. Committing a crime, with full knowledge that it is a crime, is
punishable according to the standards set by the laws of
the state where the offense occurred.

God sees sin in the same manner. When a sinner
accepts Christ and has become a new person, he agrees

to turn away from sin. When a Christian, a follower of Christ, decides to engage in an activity that he knows is wrong, God says that it is sin. There are many behaviors that the unbelieving world does not see as wrong. Many things are accepted and even encouraged by non-Christians, which should have no place in the life of a follower of Christ. For this reason, it is important for a Christian to pray that God will grant wisdom to discern what is within the will of God and what is not.

With constant prayer, reading the Word of God, and making a conscious daily effort to think on the things of God, we can begin to see the world through the eyes of God. The closer one gets to God, the manners of the world become more obvious. The Holy Spirit acts like a teacher and gradually points out more and more actions that are not pleasing to God. This is how we grow as Christians. We begin to see and hear things through the eyes and ears of God. When more of God fills our lives, the attraction to the world decreases, and we begin to desire the things of God. We will never be perfect, but when we sin, it is important to immediately go to God in prayer for forgiveness.

It is also important that we do not judge others, Christian or not. For those of us who have accepted Christ, we must remember that our lives are a continual work in progress. Once we start thinking that we have arrived at a level of such accomplishment that we can judge another, we need to remember that God will judge us by the same standard with which we judge someone else.

CHAPTER SEVENTEEN

A truthful witness does not deceive, but a
false witness pours out lies.

Proverbs 14:5

As I was patrolling one night, I noticed a pick-up
truck stop abruptly near me and saw a man earnestly
attempting to get my attention. I stopped to talk to him
and realized that his shirt was covered in blood, as were
his face and hands. He told me what had happened,
and I advised him to continue on to the hospital, where
I would meet him after I had spoken to his assailant,
the suspect.

I arrested the suspect for domestic battery. The
victim, who had spoken to me on the street, was his
brother. The two had had an argument over a dog, and
it resulted in a fight. The man I arrested entered his
brother's room, pushed him into the furniture, and
punched him in the face and mouth several times. He

then had his drunken friend hold his brother down, breaking his finger in order to beat him some more.

When the trial came, the brother I arrested chose to act as his own witness and took the stand in court for himself. After catching him in several contradictory statements, the judge declared him guilty and gave him a sentence.

My father had me memorize a rhyme when I was in grade school. It went, "Oh, what a tangled web we weave, once we practice to deceive." Through the years, I would learn the incredible truth behind this simple rhyme. It is easy to remember the truth, because the story never changes. But, as my mother told me, one lie tends to build on the next, and then you have to remember all of your lies so that you don't slip up and contradict yourself when you least expect it. One thing I am thankful for is that the Word of God is truth, a solid foundation on which I can always stand.

CHAPTER EIGHTEEN

But his delight is in the law of the Lord,
and on His law he meditates day and night.
Psalm 1:2

I stopped a car one night for speeding. The car stop resulted in the arrest of the driver for DUI, but there were a few other charges as well.

When I approached the vehicle, I asked the driver, a female over thirty years of age, for her driver's license and insurance. In her state of intoxication, she handed me an expired insurance paper and her electric bill. When I asked her for her name and date of birth, she gave me a birth date that would have made her twelve years old. After the woman became belligerent, refusing to perform the sobriety tests, I arrested her for DUI and brought her to the jail. Because there had been an open, cold beer in the front console next to her, she was also charged with "Transportation of Open Container."

It is against the law in Kansas to operate a vehicle with an open container of any alcoholic beverage in the driver's compartment.

Due to the numerous charges I needed to write on the citations and arrest reports for this case, I was glad that I had a book that gave me the statute violation numbers. Having read many of these statutes hundreds of times in the past, I knew exactly where some of them could be found. Others were a little more obscure, and so the book came in handy. It is always an excellent idea to review the laws on a frequent basis.

It is of vital importance for a Christian to memorize Scripture and meditate on the laws of God continually. When evil tempts us, God promises that his Word is sharper than any two-edged sword, and it is ours to use against the powers of darkness. In order to be able to use it quickly in the time of need, we must be familiar with it. It is a concealed weapon, which we do not need a permit to carry.

CHAPTER NINETEEN

You, my brothers, were called to be free. But
do not use your freedom to indulge the sinful nature; rather, serve one another in love.

Galatians 5:13

On many police cars are written the words "To Protect
and Serve," or a variation of the same phrase. We, as law
enforcement, are referred to as "public servants" and are
called upon to perform a multitude of functions. I have
worn many hats as a police officer and have often been
amazed that many people see us as the ones they can
call no matter what they need. I have assisted residents
with water leakage problems, answered questions about
pets, responded to calls about heaters, and yes, even
rescued cats from trees. Police work isn't always about
fighting crime, writing citations, and making arrests.
The "serve" part covers a broad category and tends to
be viewed as the less intriguing part of the job. I feel

that it is an honor to be part of a profession where the public trusts us just because of the uniform we wear.

Christ calls us to serve one another on a daily basis. This can be accomplished in many different ways. Random acts of kindness, choosing to do something nice to an individual who has wronged us, putting someone else's interests above our own, helping when we are able to be of assistance, and giving to those who are in need are all examples of serving. Jesus was a perfect example of someone who gave everything, including his life, in order to serve the needs of a sinful, undeserving world. As a result of his servant role, we are able to have eternal life in heaven.

Lord, give me the courage to be a servant, so that I can be more effective for you at work and in my everyday life.

CHAPTER TWENTY

Even though I walk through the valley of
the shadow of death, I will fear no evil, for
you are with me ...

Psalm 23:4A

Since 1792, over 17,000 police officers have been killed
in the line of duty. Approximately every fifty-three and
a half hours, an officer dies while performing his job
responsibilities. This equates to about 163 law enforcement deaths every year. Statistics state that 56,000
police officers are assaulted every year, resulting in
about 16,000 injuries.

When I attended the police academy, I was amazed
to hear an instructor encourage the class to have faith
in God. He stated that, if we didn't already trust in
God, we were entering a profession where it would be
in our best interest to put our trust in him. This espe-
cially caught my interest because this was not a Chris-

tian learning institution. The police program was part of a secular state university.

Although the knowledge that this is a dangerous job is always in the back of my mind, I do not allow this knowledge to infringe on the performance of my duties. I exercise caution and do my best to avoid complacency; however, I am aware that even the most seasoned officer can encounter the unexpected.

Prayer is an important part of the work day or work night. The spirit of fear is not from the Lord, and I am thankful that he walks with me every step I take.

CHAPTER TWENTY-ONE

Your word is a lamp to my feet and a light
for my path.

Psalm 119:105

Working the full-time midnight shift, I have found
that police work is impossible without my flashlight.
I use my flashlight to illuminate a person's face when
I am performing a DUI investigation. I use it to shine
into a driver's compartment during a car stop so that I
can see the location of the driver's hands, monitor his
movements, and ensure that there are no weapons or
contraband items in the vehicle. I need my flashlight
to conduct searches and to cast light on my surroundings when I am walking in dark areas. I use it to produce quick, intermittent bursts of light when I am con-
ducting a search in a potentially dangerous scenario. I
also use it to assist with traffic flow at the scene of car
wrecks and cast light on a house when I am searching

for an address. As a police officer, I simply cannot perform my job effectively without my flashlight.

The Word of God is the most important tool that a Christian possesses. With proper knowledge of the Word of God, which comes through studying it faithfully, we can find the answers to all of life's questions. In God's Word, there are solutions for problems of daily living, challenges for Christian growth, and advice for relationships. In it, we can find peace during times of struggle, hope for anxiety, and encouragement when the concerns of this life seem overwhelming. The Word of God gives us direction, correction, and strength. It points the way for us to go and shines light when there is darkness. As followers of Christ, we simply cannot live our lives effectively without the Word of God.

CHAPTER TWENTY-TWO

Abstain from all appearance of evil.

1 Thessalonians 5:22 (KJV)

I was sitting in a semi-hidden spot one morning, observing traffic and operating radar. The pastor of the church where I attended pulled up beside the patrol car in his personal vehicle and greeted me. Usually, he got up early in the morning to get a cappuccino and head to the church. I saw him fairly regularly at this hour, so it did not surprise me when he stopped to chat with me for a few minutes. I had not attended church the previous Sunday and still had a monetary gift in my wallet for missions, which I intended to give. I asked the pastor if it would be okay for me to give it to him then, and he stated that it would be fine. As I stretched my arm out of the patrol car window, with the money in my hand, I noticed oncoming traffic. I immediately withdrew my hand and jokingly told the pastor, "It would probably be better if I waited for the traffic to pass first."

We laughed as he stated, "It would look even worse if I was handing you the money!"

As a police officer, I find it necessary to keep a constant check on my conduct in public. Everything that I do and say is a reflection on the police department where I work. As I represent the law enforcement field, everything that I say and do also has an effect on the reputation of the police profession. This actually holds true for all occupations. There are certain vocations, such as law enforcement and teachers, which carry a standard of moral conduct. Obviously, this is not always adhered to, but the trust of the public depends on good personal character within every profession.

As a representative of Jesus Christ, it is important to be constantly mindful of my words and deeds. The world is watching, and sometimes my life is the only Jesus some people will ever see or know. As a member of the body of Christ, I have to avoid even the appearance of evil. I will never be perfect, and mistakes will happen, but the unbelieving world is more interested in my actions than in my words.

CHAPTER TWENTY-THREE

There is a way that seems right to a man,
but in the end it leads to death.

Proverbs 14:12

Many times, during the process of arresting a drunk driver, I am met with the phrase, "I haven't done anything wrong." I vividly recall one time when the corrections officer at the jail questioned my arrestee on his actions that night, and the man responded that he didn't think that drinking and driving was wrong.

Some of the statistics on drunk driving are staggering. According to the statistics cited on the Mothers against Drunk Driving (MADD) Web site (www.madd.org):

1. There were 12,998 deaths in 2007 from drunk driving.

2. There is about one death every forty minutes from drunk driving.

3. In 2001, there were over a half
   a million injuries as a result of
   alcohol related crashes.

4. In 2002, there were over 159
   million incidences of driving
   while impaired by alcohol.

5. Unfortunately, working the midnight
   shift allows me to personally experience
   one other drunken driving statistic:
   According to page four of the MADD
   Web site, "seventy-five percent of
   the fatal crashes between midnight
   and 3 a.m. involve alcohol."

It is no wonder that the Word of God gives such a bold warning about the abuse of alcohol. The ways of the world without Christ promise pleasure for a short time. The end results of these pleasures are self destruction and ultimately death. When someone decides to follow Christ, that individual becomes a brand new person. The old sinful ways die, but there is new life in Christ. This lifelong relationship with Jesus is a constant building process. The better we know him, the more we learn to walk in his ways. A Christian is never perfect, but when a Christian sins, thank God that his forgiveness and restoration are just a prayer away.

CHAPTER
TWENTY-FOUR

For I am convinced that neither death nor
life, neither angels nor demons, neither the
present nor the future, nor any powers, neither height nor depth, nor anything else in all
creation, will be able to separate us from the
love of God that is in Christ Jesus our Lord.

Romans 8:38–39

Normally, several times a night, the county dispatchers
will call out my badge number, and say, "Ten-seven-
teen?" This is police language for asking me if I am
okay. If I make a vehicle stop that takes longer than
usual, or if I am involved in a potentially volatile situation, every few minutes I am fortunate to have this
radio transmitted check on the status of my well-being.
If I fail to answer the check, or if I respond with anything other than "ten-four," signifying that I am fine,
several deputies or police cars will head my direction at

top speed with lights and sirens. I have been in situations where the distant sound of the approaching sirens or the sight of flashing police car lights was a welcome relief. It is encouraging to know that, for the most part, back-up is only a radio transmission away. There are times when it is not feasible for help to arrive as quickly as I would like, but thankfully, that is not the norm.

I am extremely thankful that anytime I call on the Lord, he is already there to help me. When I prayed to God, accepted Jesus Christ as my Savior, and gave him control over my life, I became inseparable from him. Even if the storms of everyday life rage, and death itself knocks on my door, my mind can rest in perfect peace. There is nothing that God cannot handle. My life is safe in the hands of the Creator of the Universe. It is a powerful thing to be completely sure that even when my time on this earth is over, my soul will be in heaven forever with Christ, who watches over all of his children.

CHAPTER TWENTY-FIVE

"Come, follow me," Jesus said.

Matthew 4:19A

I was talking to an informant one night at the police department. He was intoxicated and grew slightly disorderly. Challenging me to fight him, he said, "Take that badge off, and you wouldn't last five minutes out here on these streets!" I was humored by his proclamation, because, whether I wear a badge, a police shirt, or merely a t-shirt and jeans, I am still a police officer. The clothes do not make me what I am. The consequence of the informant having a physical confrontation with me while I am off duty would still result in a trip to the county jail.

To be a Christian is to be a follower of Christ and to be like Christ. Although we will never achieve the perfection of Jesus, our goal as Christians should be to daily pray that God would give us the characteristics, reactions, and attitudes of Jesus. Many people wear bracelets that read, "What Would Jesus Do?" That question should be constantly in our thoughts and displayed in our efforts.

Many things in this world are labeled as "Christian," but actually have nothing to do with true Christianity. Music, books, people, and even religions are often wrongfully given the world's stamp of being Christian. Our actions of truly following Christ and striving to be like him, and living in honest, passionate, wholehearted pursuit of him make us Christians, not the clothes we wear, the words we speak, or the fact that we attend church.

Although it is fantastic when the rest of the world thinks that we must be Christians, our final stamp of approval needs to be from God. Jesus himself gave us the directions for true Christianity when he said, "Follow me."

CHAPTER TWENTY-SIX

Yet to all who received Him, to those who
believed in His name, He gave the right to
become children of God.

John 1:12

I remember sitting in the classroom while I was still
in the police academy, listening to the instructor as he
put out a challenge to the room. He told us that some
of us would not make it through the program and that
most of us who *did* successfully complete the program
would never get jobs in law enforcement. We were also
told that, among those of us who did get jobs, most
would leave the field within the first few years. The
challenge then, to the classroom of police cadets, was,
were we willing to stay in the program and do our best
to succeed and become police officers, or were we going
to quit? The odds were against me, but I accepted the
challenge and finished the program ranked fifth in

my class, earning the right to become a police officer. When I stepped into a patrol car and put the keys in the ignition for the first time as a commissioned officer, it was the proudest moment of my life.

There are over six billion people in this world. Millions have never heard the gospel of Jesus Christ. Many millions more have heard of Jesus and believe that he existed, but have no idea what it means to have a relationship with him. Then, unfortunately, many millions more do not have a desire to know God. This is how it has been for centuries.

It is humbling that the Creator of the universe thought it was important to find me in the middle of the world's billions and made sure that I heard his Word. I could never express my gratitude, no matter how eloquently the words flowed from my mouth. The odds weren't in my favor, but God made sure that I was given the opportunity to accept his Son and was then given the right to become a child of God.

It saddens me to know that, in this world, some will live and die and never know the truth that Jesus Christ died to save them from their sins and give them eternal life. It saddens me even more to know that some will continue to reject him, even after being told that Jesus Christ is the *only* way to heaven.

CHAPTER TWENTY-SEVEN

The heart is deceitful above all things, and
desperately wicked: who can know it?

Jeremiah 17:9

I was called out to a house one night, where an individual had run after a confrontation in an alley. The suspect, a young man in his twenties, had just stabbed another man in the alley and was now hiding in his house. I was told that he was possibly armed with a gun and would not have a problem shooting at me if he felt threatened. The man's relative, who lived next door, was able to convince him to open the door and cooperate.

The victim, also a young man in his twenties, had been sent to the hospital. The knife wound had very nearly punctured his lung, and he remained in the hospital for several days.

What drives a man to commit acts of violence against another man? A wicked heart, which does not know the love of God, cannot be expected to love a neighbor as himself, as Jesus commanded.

I thank God daily for salvation. Without the Lord, I would not be able to see things through the eyes of a new man who is alive in Christ. Without the love of God compelling me, I am well aware that I could be on the other side of the law, because the heart of man is wicked. The evil of this world and the pursuits for the temporary happiness of this world are results of the blindness of mankind to the ways of Christ. Jesus said that he is Living Water, and once we drink from God's fountain, we will never thirst for the things or the ways of this world again.

CHAPTER TWENTY-EIGHT

It [love] always protects, always trusts,
always hopes, always perseveres.

1 Corinthians 13:4A

I arrived at the home of a young lady, who had been hit in the face by her boyfriend. Her left eye was swollen, and she wanted to press criminal charges against him for battery. This was the third time she had been beaten by him.

Many times I have encountered situations just like this one. Sometimes the aggressor is a man; sometimes the man is the victim. More often than not, my experience has been that after arresting the suspect for the battery, the two who were involved in the dispute get back together again and drop the charges in court. Obviously, this is not always the case, but it is a common story across the nation. The average victim of a domestic battery makes seven attempts at leaving the abuser before finally ending the relationship.

True love is not violent; it does not seek to hurt; it does not place its own interests above the well-being of another. Battery, as a result of a jealous or angry rage, is not a product of true love.

The purest example of true love was God himself, giving an undeserving, unloving, unbelieving world the gift of his only Son in order that sinners could enter heaven's gates. When we accept God's love, it protects us from an eternity of separation from him. When we trust in the love of Jesus Christ, we are given the splendor of heaven. When we live in the light of God's love here on earth, we have hope when the rest of the world would normally give up hope. When we know there is the prize of an everlasting crown in heaven after this life is over, it gives us incentive to persevere in God's love. The love of God is perfect. Lord, teach us to love one another the way you taught us to love.

CHAPTER
TWENTY-NINE

When I was a child, I talked like a child. I thought like a child. I had the understanding of a child. When I became a man, I put childish ways behind me.

1 Corinthians 13:11

I was in the police car one night, when a vehicle stopped next to me near a stop light. A lady was driving with her little boy in the front passenger seat. The little boy rolled his window down and asked me how fast the police car could go and if I wanted to race. When I nicely declined, he asked me, "Have you shot anybody yet?" Before I could answer, he stated, "Because that's the cool part."

As a child, I gave little thought to the fact that life itself is a gift from God, which he continues to give every day. The Bible says that every good and perfect gift comes from God. Life is a good gift. When God created life, he called it "good." But his perfect gift came in the form of his Son, Jesus Christ. The Son of God, in human form, was sent here to rescue mankind from the certainty of eternal spiritual death. The very thought of this is more than the mind can fathom.

As I have grown older, my understanding and appreciation of the gifts of God have grown stronger. I am grateful for every day that the Lord wakes me up to do his work. When I accepted salvation through Christ, I finally knew the answer to, "Why am I here?" The years may slip by more quickly than they did when I was a child, but I now realize that I, along with every Christian, have a divine purpose to accomplish. My mission is to tell as many people as possible about Jesus and be a working member of the body of Christ here on earth.

The body has two hands, two feet, two ears, but only one mouth. It is important that I listen twice as hard to hear the voice of the Lord. After listening, I must urge my feet on "double-time" to go where he sends me. When he gives me a job, my two hands should be working harder than my mouth, so that my actions speak louder than my words in a language the world understands.

God's Word says that his harvest is plentiful, but the laborers are few.

Lord, help me to encourage others to be a working part of your body here on earth.

CHAPTER THIRTY

When I say to the wicked, "O wicked man,
you will surely die," and you do not speak
out to dissuade him from his ways, that
wicked man will die for his sin, and I will
hold you accountable for his blood.

Ezekiel 33:8

An intoxicated young man stepped out of the driver's
side of his vehicle at my request early one morning in
order to perform the required sobriety tests. Knowing
that he was too impaired to successfully complete the
tests and that he was going to jail for drunk driving, he
earnestly asked me to allow him to drive away, assuring
me that he was headed straight home. I told him that I
could not do that and continued with the arrest proce-
dure and brought him to the jail.

Some things are left to "officer discretion." The reasoning behind this is that, if I make a bad decision while using "officer discretion" and allow an impaired individual to drive away, the intoxicated driver could possibly cause a fatal accident. At that point, the blame for the fatality would fall on me for knowingly allowing a drunk driver to operate a motor vehicle. I am not held liable for every drunk driver out on the roads, but have a duty to act on the ones I encounter.

Jesus commanded us, as Christians, to go to the ends of the earth, making sure that everyone hears the good news of salvation. It was a command, not a request. It is important that we pray, asking the Lord for boldness in sharing Christ with others. Some are ashamed to bring up the name of Jesus Christ to their unsaved friends. We live in a society where Christ is not seen as a serious answer to life's problems, the Bible is not the ultimate source for tough issues, and the words "I'll pray for you" are often just cliché. Some are afraid that, if they witness to people about Jesus, they will be laughed at, ridiculed, or ostracized. We must remember that when Jesus was here and told the world, "I am the way," he was treated in the same manner.

But most importantly, the Bible gives a warning. When we know that a friend or relative has not heard the message of salvation and we deliberately do not witness to them about Christ, God holds us partially accountable for their spiritual loss. If we try to witness to them and they do not accept God's free gift of salvation, the accountability is their own. We cannot exercise "discretion" and pick and choose who should hear about God. The Lord made it mandatory for us to witness to the lost. We are not liable for the entire world, but we do have a duty to act on the ones we encounter.

CHAPTER THIRTY-ONE

A gentle answer turns away wrath, but a harsh word stirs up anger.

Proverbs 15:1

Before entering the law enforcement academy, I was sure that the police defense tactics classes would teach me how to take any bull by the horns and crumple him to the ground by sheer force and physical technique. Little did I expect that, on the first class in this field, I would be learning how to treat people as if they were my own family.

Respectfulness, courtesy, a civil tone, friendliness, and treating people how I would want to be treated would deter hundreds of physical confrontations. The idea of it made sense but sounded like typical classroom rhetoric that held no truth once tested out in the real world. Would this be yet another case where, once I was out on the street, senior officers would tell me,

"Forget what you learned about that. What they teach you in the classroom and what goes on in the real world are two different things"?

Obviously, not everyone responds the same way, and there are those who require more firm treatment in order to gain compliance; however, even that can be done respectfully. I have been amazed at the number of times I have been thanked after bringing a prisoner to the jail. Quite a few have commented that, although they have had many encounters with law enforcement, they were not always treated in a civil manner. Some of these same people have stated that normally they would have tried to fight with me, but when they were confronted in a friendly way, they changed their minds.

It is a simple and short truth, yet profound. A soft word, an understanding attitude, and politeness shown to most people can diffuse many explosive situations. I have probably used this Biblical truth more than any other in my police career. Once again, the Word of God stands true and is practical for everyday use.

CHAPTER THIRTY-TWO

I therefore, the prisoner of the Lord, beseech you that ye walk worthy of the vocation wherewith ye are called.

Ephesians 4:1 (KJV)

When I took an oath to protect the community in which I serve, I took on a specific vocation. My job, just like every occupation, has definite expectations that are required of me. I am expected to assist citizens in upholding the local city statutes, protect the community, and make decisions involving consequences for those who violate the laws of peaceful society. If, at any time, I choose not to adhere to the guidelines of my job, I can be terminated. The same holds true for any profession. Every employer wants an excellent staff. Every employee, no matter what his job is, can take pride at the end of the day knowing that he has done his best and has produced the best efforts possible. By striving to be the best in our workplace, we show that we are worthy of our vocation.

God calls us, as Christians, to conduct ourselves in a manner that is worthy of the vocation to which he has called us. Although we may have full-time jobs in this world, we also have full-time jobs in God's work. Some of us are called to be apostles, some are prophets, some are evangelists, some are pastors, and others are teachers. It is our responsibility to perform our function in God's work as it says in Ephesians 4:12, "For the perfecting of the saints, for the work of the ministry, for the edifying of the body of Christ." These responsibilities are to be performed with intense dedication and are not to be taken lightly. The same God who gave us our vocation has all authority to terminate our involvement in any mission that we fail to give our full efforts. Lord, help me to walk worthy of the vocation you have given me, and perform my part with excellence.

CHAPTER THIRTY-THREE

The wind blows wherever it pleases. You
hear its sound, but you can not tell where
it comes from or where it is going. So it is
with everyone born of the Spirit.

John 3:8

A pastor had asked for representatives of the police
department to give a presentation at his church one
Sunday night, and, after receiving permission from
my chief, I prepared a surprise for the congregation.
Although I arrived in a police car and was dressed in
full uniform, I spoke to the church as a Christian officer, sharing my faith in Jesus Christ. They were pleased
to know that my relationship with Christ is on top of
my priority list.

While speaking to them, I asked, "When you think
of a police officer, what is the first thing that comes to
your mind?" The responses were not unexpected; tickets

and jail were the most popular. The subject of speeding tickets, although it is never humorous to be on the receiving end of one, usually creates a few laughs.

How do I know how fast a vehicle is going? How do I know whether a driver is speeding excessively over the posted speed limit? The answer is simple: radar. Radar is something that invisibly detects how fast an object is moving. Radar cannot be seen. Radar can work in several different directions, regardless of which way the police car is facing at the time the radar is in use. There are many devices to detect radar. Some of them work; some do not. For the most part, the average driver does not know if radar is being utilized to detect the speed of his or her vehicle. Use of excessive speed, detected by invisible radar, often will result in a citation for speeding.

The Holy Spirit cannot be seen. However, the spirit of God leads us in the direction we need to go, when we are obedient to God's will. My prayer is that my life will be filled with less of me and more of the Holy Spirit. A life led by the spirit of God results in certain obviously detectable behaviors known as the fruit of the Spirit. In Galatians 5:22, the apostle Paul tells us what some of these fruits are: love, joy, peace, patience, kindness, goodness, faithfulness, gentleness, and self-control. A person who is filled with the Holy Spirit will have some, if not all, of these traits. It is no wonder then that Christians are considered to be different by the world's standards.

CHAPTER
THIRTY-FOUR

Many are the plans in a man's heart, but it
is the Lord's purpose that prevails.

Proverbs 19:21

There is a juvenile facility for girls in my area of jurisdiction. The main purpose of this place is to give girls a
final chance to change their negative behavioral patterns
before their actions result in incarceration in a juvenile
detention center. Unfortunately, it is not uncommon
for me to be called there for reports of fighting among
the residents. But, more commonly, my involvement
with this facility is to attempt to locate resident girls
who have run away in an effort to escape the system.
Although, on a rare occasion, one of the girls succeeds
in running away, more often than not, they are caught
by law enforcement and returned to the facility.

I remember one specific occasion when three girls
ran at once. They had been gone for a few hours by the

time my shift began. The three girls devised their own agenda of plans, but when two of them approached a local resident of the community and asked him for cigarettes, they were surprised when he informed them that he was a police officer. They were held until I arrived and took them into custody. Within minutes, the third one had been caught as well, when she tried to convince a local business owner to drive her out of town. The system is meant to help them, but many fight against it.

I have discovered that true happiness only comes from following the instructions of the Lord. Real inner peace only comes from being obedient to his leading. It is of no value to struggle against the will of God. Jonah attempted this and found himself in the belly of a large fish for three days. Ultimately, the purpose of the Lord prevailed. God is looking for a willing heart to carry out his purposes. When we give up our stubbornness and submit our lives to Christ, then we can truly live.

CHAPTER THIRTY-FIVE

Train a child in the way he should go, and
when he is old he will not turn from it.

Proverbs 22:6

I stopped a vehicle one night for several traffic violations. The driver, a minor, had been drinking, and I arrested him for DUI. His blood alcohol concentration was four times the maximum legal limit for a driver of his age. When I asked him where he had been drinking, he told me that he had been getting drunk with his mother and some other company in a hotel room. Although some states allow minors to drink in the presence of a parent or guardian, no state condones a parent permitting a child to drive while intoxicated.

I know of parents who have smoked marijuana with their children and parents who have even given their children tips on which meth cooks and dealers are better than others. I listened to a story from a girl who said that, at the age of twelve, she was sold to different men in exchange for cigarettes for her mother. I have been in homes where inappropriate language was acceptable conversation between a parent and a child. I have heard complaints from children who referred to the bar as their parent's "second home." In every city, there are many children living with their parents in filthy, drug infested houses. I have often thought, *What a difference God could make here.*

I thank God that I was raised in a home with Christian parents. However, children who are not raised with a godly example also have the capability of retaining negative behaviors learned in the home during childhood years. A child who is given a negative example and taught by his parents that certain crimes are acceptable behavior has an excellent chance of continuing that behavior. Many times, I have heard police officers state that they have grown tired of going to calls where a parent cannot control the child. Sometimes, parents ask me to "scare their child into thinking they are going to jail," in hopes that the child will "straighten up." I decline these requests.

The Word of God is a powerful tool for parents and children. Fortunately, the Bible has advice for both when it says in 2 Timothy 3:14–17, "But as for you, continue in what you have learned and have become convinced of, because you know those from whom you learned it, and how from infancy you have known the holy Scriptures, which are able to make you wise for salvation through faith in Christ Jesus. All Scripture is God-breathed and is useful for teaching, rebuking, correcting and training in righteousness, so that the man of God may be thoroughly equipped for every good work."

This is proof enough that we, as the hands, feet, eyes, ears, and mouth of Christ, need to do our part in the work which God has commissioned us to do. No one is too old or too young to hear the saving, life changing message of Jesus Christ.

CHAPTER THIRTY-SIX

Put on the full armor of God so that you can
take your stand against the devil's schemes.
Ephesians 6:11

Once in a great while, as I am getting ready for work,
I think how odd it is that I actually put on a bullet-
proof vest as a daily part of my job's attire. However,
the thought of whether or not I will come home the
following morning does not enter my mind. I generally
do not give it a second thought, as I put on a belt with
various weapons, including a forty-caliber handgun.
These items are all an essential part of my job; I need
them in order to effectively perform my duties to the
fullest capacity. Without them, I cannot carry out my
responsibilities with complete power and competence.

The armor of God is the same. Ephesians six gives
a complete list of the armor of God: the belt of truth,
the breastplate of righteousness, feet shod with the

readiness of the gospel, the shield of faith, the helmet of salvation, and the sword of the Spirit. Along with these vital pieces of armor, we are to pray and stay alert. We simply cannot perform our daily functions in the kingdom of God without his full armor. If we neglect one piece, we make ourselves open to a successful attack from the enemy and cannot carry out our responsibilities as Christians with power and competence.

Lord, I ask that, every day, I would be fitted with your full armor so that I can withstand the spiritual attacks from the enemy, and perform my duties as a soldier in your army.

CHAPTER
THIRTY-SEVEN

I am the vine; you are the branches. If a man
remains in me and I in him, he will bear much
fruit; apart from me you can do nothing.

John 15:5

In December of 2007, the city where I work was hit by
a major ice storm. As the ice accumulated, power poles
snapped and trees toppled. Electric lines were strewn
around the streets and lawns like spaghetti; large limbs
crushed roofs of houses and damaged vehicles, and
the city was without power for a week. Streets were
impassable as branches, heavily laden with ice, were
bent down into the roadways.

I remember thinking, *When July comes, we probably won't even be able to tell that this mess was ever here.*
The damage took months to clear. Power companies
restored electric service to homes, construction crews

worked on houses, and tree service companies had more than enough to stay very busy.

The trees, although they had been severely damaged in the ice storm, remained strong and healthy. Broken limbs and branches, split from the main trunks of trees, were cut up and stacked neatly into kindling piles. Large limbs, no longer attached to the trees, would soon dry and die and be useful only for firewood. But the trees themselves bloomed in the spring, and new growth appeared in time. By summertime the thick, green leaves almost allowed no remembrance of the winter storm.

Christ said that he is the vine. When we, the branches, are connected to the vine, we have access to the living water of Christ and can feed our souls on the bread of life. We are able to grow and produce fruit and are a productive part of the body of Christ here on earth.

Separation from the vine renders us useless. Without constant fellowship with Christ through prayer, and a daily desire to become closer to him, we gradually die. A dead branch is not useful in the kingdom of God.

It is important that we pray daily for the Lord to draw us closer to him, to be filled with the Holy Spirit, and to be obedient to the tasks he has for us to perform. We all have talents, and we all have a job to do in God's kingdom. Any time we are unsure of our duties, we simply need to pray and ask him to show us what he needs us to do. It is important that we remain as useful branches.

CHAPTER THIRTY-EIGHT

Pure religion and undefiled before God and the Father is this, To visit the fatherless and the widows in their affliction and to keep himself unspotted from the world.

James 1:27 (KJV)

It was late one dark night. I was in a very different type of police attire on this particular night. Dressed completely in black, I was with my assistant chief, silently observing a meth house. Having parked an unmarked police truck a few blocks away, we silently moved through the shadows of the back alleys until we could clearly observe the house. It was rumored that someone inside the residence had night vision goggles, so when a figure appeared at an upstairs door, peering our direction into the alleyway, we laid facedown, flat on the ground, until the person was gone. We had successfully blended in with our surroundings, unspotted from the potential danger.

Unfortunately, many people professing to be Christians feel the need to blend in with the world in order not to be labeled as followers of Jesus. Christians are often seen as strange, or maybe even fanatics, having little in common with the everyday man of the world. Paul makes sure to let us know in Ephesians 2:19, "Consequently, you are no longer foreigners and strangers, but fellow citizens with God's people and also members of His household." Professing to be a follower of Christ is not something to hide; it is not shameful to be on the winning side!

Some Christians feel it is necessary to look, act, and sound like the world in order to be accepted by the world. Then, when the world accepts them, they believe that they can "minister" to the lost. But, if the unbeliever can see no difference between the saved and the lost man, he indeed will feel little incentive to accept Christ. Some Christians seem to have the need to remain incognito and want to blend in perfectly with the rest of the unbelieving world. The harsh reality of this scenario is that God cannot use a Christian who will not stand up for him.

Most importantly, a reluctant, embarrassed Christian attempting to not be spotted and labeled as a follower of Jesus is doing the exact opposite of what James said when he stated that we are to be unspotted by the world. A Christian trying to remain unspotted from the world is one who will not conform to ungodly ways, but continues to be lead by the Holy Spirit. The Lord demands that we be different form the world. This is supported in Scripture when the Apostle Paul writes, "Therefore, come out from them, and be separate, says the Lord ... " (2 Corinthians 6:17a).

As Christians, we cannot camouflage ourselves and blend in with this world. We are commanded to be different.

CHAPTER THIRTY-NINE

But whoever listens to me will live in safety
and be at ease, without fear of harm.

Proverbs 1:33

I remember arriving at a house early one morning, along with several other police cars. We were the entry team, getting ready to raid a house where meth was being manufactured. We quickly gathered in formation at the back door. The lead man kicked in the door, and we entered the home, shouting, "Police department! Search warrant!" We seized a meth lab. Parked on the side of the house was a pick-up truck, its bed filled to nearly overflowing with black trash bags. From inside of the trash bags, we gathered piles of waste from the meth lab and many needles which had been used for injecting the illegal substance.

It is becoming common practice for meth cooks to leave booby traps inside of their houses in order to deter invasions such as the one above. Everything from poisonous gases that explode from light bulbs when the light switch is turned on, to rattlesnakes and vipers let loose in the house can be used as a surprise waiting for any intruder wishing to arrive without warning. These criminal methods of protecting the illegal meth labs have sent many law enforcement officers to the emergency room.

How difficult it must be to live in constant fear, unrest, and paranoia. Many caught up in this lifestyle have described episodes where they went for weeks without sleep. The lack of sleep, combined with the constant usage of drugs, eventually propels the mind into a delusional mode, filled with its own fearful unreality. A person in this state can be very dangerous.

Jesus offers rest. As a follower of Christ, I have no fear of death, and even when life throws negativity in my direction, I am perfectly confident that the Lord can handle it. There is no concern too great for God. 1 Peter 5:7 says, "Cast all your anxiety on him because he cares for you."

Jesus also offers a purpose for living. When someone gives their life to Christ, that person can begin a new life. God can use the new believer to bring others into his kingdom, and with a new outlook and higher purpose, the changed individual can contribute to a better society.

Jesus offers peace. When I gave my life to Christ, I found perfect peace. If I am troubled by anything, it is an automatic reflex to take it to the Lord in prayer. Thank you, Lord, for the rest, purpose, and peace you give to those who trust in You.

CHAPTER FORTY

But be ye doers of the word, not hearers
only, deceiving your own selves."
                                    James 1:22 (KJV)

I heard over the radio one night that a county sheriff deputy was chasing a vehicle into the city of my
jurisdiction. Two patrol cars, including mine, joined
in the attempt to stop the suspect vehicle. When the
sheriff car and the other city police car went one way,
I cut around to a different block in an effort to box in
the suspect's vehicle. Instead of stopping, the suspect
accelerated his pick-up truck into a head-on collision
course with my patrol car. I swerved at the last second
to avoid the crash and continued around to the next
block. The careless driver came back around again, and
I made another attempt at boxing him between all of
the patrol cars by placing my car nearly sideways across
the road, in an effort to block his forward progress.

Again, instead of stopping, he accelerated into another crash course aimed at my driver's side door. I pulled forward to avoid the collision once more. He drove by me and pulled into a driveway behind my vehicle. I exited my car and removed him from his truck. The aroma of marijuana was prominent when I opened his door. He staggered out of the vehicle, very intoxicated, and made an aggressive move in my direction, suggestive of an imminent fight. He was quickly brought to the ground by a taser, and another officer and I handcuffed him. I immediately recognized the man as an individual I had dealt with the year before this incident for drunk driving. Obviously, he had not learned anything from his previous jail experience. He had heard the warnings of the law; he had even experienced the consequences of breaking the same law, yet he had chosen not to learn anything from it.

Sometimes I wonder, *How many times do our ears listen to the Word of God before we finally hear it? How many times can we quote a verse by memory or read a passage of Scripture without really hearing what God is saying to us?*

It is necessary to pay strict attention to every word of Scripture as we read it and truly attempt to grasp its full meaning by heeding the prompting of the Holy Spirit as the Lord ministers to us through his written Word. I think some Christians become obsessed with the quantity of Scripture that they read, as opposed to the quality of the time spent reading God's Word. God speaks to us through his written word, as well as through other people. Although it is noble to read through the

Bible in a year, do not shrug off the prompting of the Holy Spirit to linger a bit longer on a certain scripture. Sometimes the Lord tells me to stop reading and meditate on what I have read, because there is something specific he wants to tell me.

As we read the Bible, we must pray, "Speak, Lord, for your servant is listening." Then, when he speaks through his Word, we must be doers of the Word and put what we have learned into action. If we don't, then we are merely hearers of the Word, deceiving ourselves, having not learned what he wanted us to learn.

CONCLUSION

Every day we have opportunities to view our experiences and circumstances with a spiritual perspective. If we take a few steps back and look at the entire picture, keeping our eternal goals in the forefront of our minds, we find that many things just aren't worth the worry and stress that we, as humans, tend to give. It isn't always an easy task to put aside our human tendencies and allow God complete control over the details of our lives, but with daily prayer, this task eventually becomes second nature.

It is important to study and memorize Scripture in order to be able to recall the words of Christ as we live our everyday lives. In every encounter, our reactions should reflect the very scriptures that we have hidden in our hearts.

Quiet devotional time dedicated to hearing God's voice will enable us to see spiritual lessons in circumstances that would normally be easily overlooked. To the non-believer, these words are senseless. Jesus said that those who seek him would find him. As you embark on a new relationship with Christ, I encourage you to pray, asking God to give you a new life, forgiveness from the chains of sin, freedom from the slavery of addictions, and peace beyond comprehension. Jesus Christ will be with you throughout this life to encourage you in times of darkness, to share your joy in times of triumph and victory, to give you hope where there seems to be none, to walk with you through the curtains of death, and to embrace you as you spend eternity with him in heaven. There is no greater comfort than to know God in a personal way and to spend this life developing that relationship, assured that victory is yours.

To those seeking to know God in a closer relationship, I pray that this book has given you an example of how to exercise your spiritual sight. I have given you a small sample of experiences from my law enforcement life. I pray that we persist in learning the eternal lessons from our everyday lives and continually seek to see things his way.